Altered States

To those who came,
and those they found here.

Catherine Fisher
Altered States

seren

seren is the book imprint of
Poetry Wales Press Ltd
2 Wyndham Street, Bridgend, Wales, CF31 1EF

© Catherine Fisher, 1999

The right of Catherine Fisher to be identified as
the author of this work has been asserted in accordance
with the Copyright, Designs and Patents Act, 1988

A CIP record for this title is available
from the British Library

ISBN 1-85411-273-2

All rights reserved. No part of this publication
may be reproduced, stored in a retrieval system,
or transmitted at any time or by any means,
electronic, mechanical, photocopying, recording
or otherwise without the prior permission of the author.

*The publisher works with the financial assistance of the
Arts Council of Wales*

Cover Art:
Detail of unrestored Icon by Cimabue, tempera on panel, Florence,
Museo dell'Opera di Santa Croce

Printed in Palatino
by WBC Book Manufacturers, Bridgend

Contents

7	Cimabue's Crucifix
8	On the Tower, Hereford
9	Altered States
10	On Grey Hill
11	Amnesia
	I Tell me anything you can remember.
12	II Learning to write.
13	III To his wife.
14	IV Out alone.
15	V First snow.
16	VI How's the reading coming?
17	Undertakers
18	The White Ship
20	Life Class I–V
25	Artist, Neath Abbey
26	At the Villa Borghese I–III
29	Mr Bucknall's Skeleton
30	Bryn-Celli-Ddu
31	Cromlech
32	Fimbulwinter
33	At Bertholey House
34	Cat Lane
35	Four Fragments for Lent
	I Tithe Barn, Llantarnam
36	II Electric Superstore
37	III Rome; Marathon
38	IV Tor
39	Vampire Ballet
40	Gipsy Horses
41	Eilmer of Malmesbury
42	The Thicket
43	Blodeuwedd
44	Re-Enactment
49	Estuary Poems I–XIV
63	*Acknowledgements*

Cimabue's Crucifix

Damaged in the Florence floods, 1966.

The water wears his hands; furrows his face.
It seeps into the wood of him, cracks and seams
swelling, splitting the still boards.
Slowly it infiltrates his beauty, lifting
gold leaf with infinite patience, flake
by flake; soaking the pigments away.

Water opens him. He's saturated,
running into long unwinding colours,
downward bruises, red and ochre;
shoulders sagging under the sopping weight.
Faces of saints, all the long night,
chin on palms, fragment in sympathy.

They're together now, loosened, dissolved;
so mingled that they'll never be apart.
The long work's over, he's come down, become
gold scum, splinters, one painted eye
floating in the wave-slap of the nave.
Outside, the world's a dripping day,

the city soaked and grey, and he slips
into the drains of it, the streets and alleyways,
the stinking houses; out of the hoses
slinking through hopeless hands. On
the walls of drowned piazzas a gold smear
marks the heights to which he's risen.

On the Tower, Hereford

Climbing the stairs, the tight turns
are an idea you can never grasp,
twisting into darkness. Legs ache,
the wall is cold; echoes shuffle
from somewhere far ahead. Always,
there's someone up ahead.

Climbing the lantern, edging round
a crack in stone. Under my toes
people hum in the nave's spaces.
Angels hang here, dusty.
This is pride, this is folly.
If no-one wants to pass me I'll be safe.

Climbing the ladders. They lean
on vaults, a cage of timbers.
Names and dates cut them deep.
Crawl here, the roof over you,
weight of wood on your shoulders.
The door tiny, like a tomb's.

Through it. The leads, high, vibrating
with bells, thrum of flagpoles,
the sky blown away to Powys.
Heart pounding with words
to take down without spilling.
And no-one here; no-one ever here.

Altered States

The piece of chalk lies on the step, and every time
he passes he picks it up and draws, outlines,

nothing she can recognize. Spirals mostly, like those
cupmarks out of archaeology, the mazes

that mock us all from megaliths, simple
with withheld significance. The lump

of chalk is stolen from some downland; it powders
smoothly on the pavement in his fingers

and she's reminded of that story in the scriptures
where Christ wrote on the ground for the accusers.

They pour from him, the curving lines, as if they were the sun
or the hot afternoon turning towards dark, the spin

of his confusions winding on themselves, and now he throws
it down and looks at her and says "I wish I knew."

On Grey Hill

He tells that story with such relish. The great boar
careering over the country, Arthur's men
scattering combs and razors, hanging on like mad
to the bizarre, biting, kicking entourage.
And the land's all green and bright and sunny,
the colours clear; Portskewett and Maes-y-gwenith,
places in legend, places in the mind
that could be anything or anywhere.
Somehow primeval, untainted yet, a land
potential, glittering with myth.
His hooves plough up the motorway; he drops
the bee and wheatseed in your reeling brain;
the images cavorting over the hills
and out into the estuary's blue arms.

Amnesia

I

Tell me anything you can remember.

Giotto is a word I remember;
Led Zeppelin, a name like Debenhams.
Jess and Aklo; Chrysostom. Clovelly.
People, are they? None of them are me.
And the sound of a certain door as it closes,
the way the handle creaks, uneasily.

I remember rooms in houses, maybe
all one house, and a garden with
a river at the edge, the banks
tunnelled by voles and sand... you know,
those birds. And running down a street
behind the beating of my heart.

Nothing connects, nothing fits together;
the names and faces come and go
drifting out of darkness, and I'm guilty,
I feel I'm letting them all down, fading
out of earshot like that box-thing in the window;
I've forgotten... Yes, that's it. The radio.

II

Learning to write.

I feel a fool at this table. The pencil
shapes the letters clumsily. I press hard
and snap it. As she goes from desk to desk

I hear you yesterday to Mary on the phone.
"Sometimes I think I'm living with a stranger.
He forgets my name. The children

cry. The piano is silent." Not so. I touched
a note; it made me shudder in the dark.
Nothing's lost like memory is lost;

you can't remember what it is you can't remember.
It's a tunnel with no end, all the songs
are there, the undreamed symphonies.

I leave the angry silence on the page,
turn over, draw a small uneven house;
windows, chimneys, curtains. And no door.

III

To his wife.

Isabelle, I thought a letter would be best;
I leave it here, on the window. Has my writing
changed? It took so long to learn again,
making the shapes, fitting them to sounds.
Oddly the numbers stayed, a tumble in my mind;
McGregor says that happens very often.
I don't know you girl, don't know who you are,
what you like to eat, what music, where we met.
I've seen the wedding photos but that man
beside you might be anyone; his eyes know
secrets I never will. The contours of your skin,
the feel of you — New worlds to me. I'm an alien,
and I know you're trying not to let me know.
We'll see it through, you say; you love me.
The thing is, I don't know if I love you.
And starting again, yes, maybe, but now I'm
someone else, like the prince in the story
that I'm sounding out so slowly, a beast
without a past, a fearsome irritable thing
breaking all the taboos clumsily, and the one
you loved is lost under the spell.
Can a kiss break that, or melt the mirror-shard,
the ice that's silenced me and set me free?

IV

Out alone.

Coming to the corner of the street I stopped,
waiting for a bus to pass, but when it had
something in my mind slid down a tunnel
and I stared at all the roads in disbelief,
not knowing which was mine; the steep
hill, the lane into the fields, the hard
grit of the alley. I was lost, totally,
as if I'd never been here in my life.

And I haven't. I was born six months ago.
Which house was mine? They all seemed
alien, painted in the colours I'd have hated.
All night I walked the alleys like a shadow,
bewildered by old men watering their hostas
and football goals chalked out on garage doors,
turning abruptly into the mind's dead ends,
looking for anywhere my keys would open.

V

First snow.

When you walk it makes small crumpling noises,
crunching to a perfect footmark.
The surface pitted with tiny hollows,

clotting leaves, rabbit-tracks; a falling powder
with no wind. The sky's darker,
looks heavy. Bird-cheep's the only sound.

Until the knock and rattle at the window,
the small girls in their red coats slithering;
"Daddy?" they call, "Come out into the snow!"

Strangers, the snow's in me. White and cold
it buries all my life under its drift.
I see it for the first time, without echoes,

the way a kitten sees it, or a bird, new
and strange; dangerous. Snow. Just snow.
And the thaw, so slow, the dripping ice

drilling holes below the apple-tree,
hours long, plopping into grassy patches,
spreading at the edges, joining up

till the lawn's back, green and muddy. So
slow. Years go by and still it hasn't ended.
Small white patches loiter in the hedges.

VI

How's the reading coming?

These stories, they haven't gone. It's strange
but I come to them as friends. Even the pictures,
the wizened trees, the way that face
scowls from the trunk. In all the work
and hurry I lost them. Now they're back.
And they say all of it, the loss, the spell
that turns you into something else, that locks
you in your tower behind the thorns,
the brambles none saw sprout, asleep
for centuries, your court about you.
I'm struggling back to something overgrown,
like the hunter scrambling through the wood,
the fool that clambers down the well
to reach his own reflection.
They understood, the ones who told these tales,
knew the sleeper and the wood grow tight,
thorn in flesh, bramble around wrist,
knew the silver tower above the trees,
the great glass mountain that I'm climbing now;
the island where the giant hid his soul;
the sword-bridge; the long road back to time.

Undertakers

The baker's doorway steams like Acheron.
They eat hot rolls and pasties, shiny grease
soaking the paper so their fingers tear it;
the thin one smokes, flicking off ash.
Their coats are raven, crypt-black, but they laugh,
swap jokes, wave at a passing van.
Later they crowd the car,
running its engines so the windows trickle;
one gazes at the bookie's wistfully.

They've done their part; performed
the silent secrets no-one asks about.
Now through fiery glass the final hymn
brings them out to stamp, rub hands,
uncrease coats and faces.
They line the porch, pull on gloves,
leave the singing to others;
their tribute no emotion and firm hands,
sharing unsteadily on shoulders
the box of dark that always weighs too much,
and comes too soon.

The White Ship

The white ship sails all night out of his dreams,
her fierce figurehead drinking the cold sea.
He leans and fingers her smooth, open lips.

Spindles of ice her frosted spars,
sails crumpling, sloughing and filling
with the salt breathing of the wind.

All day he sits, talks, works, and he forgets her,
till in a window or in someone's words
comes sea-glitter, a gull's rebuke,

and in the turning of his head he's back
among creaks and whispers, the rotating wheel
that no-one grasps, the cabin with its lamp

swinging on the outspread charts.
It's those charts he never can remember;
always as he gropes for them they've gone,

leaving a sense of infinite distance;
islands marked with strange calligraphy;
and names, names he almost knows,

that tantalise but just won't come,
so that in songs or in a poem's skirl
he tries their echoes over on his tongue.

Each night he journeys on the winter ship,
hands on the ropes, feeling the spray,
living in the cracks between his days.

And where he's sailing to he doesn't know,
except that it's too late to turn back now;
that here are all the spaces of his art,

the craft he once thought he was master of,
driving him out across an endless sea,
alone under the stars; far from home.

Life Class

I

First lines are faint, even fearful.
Charcoal crumbles, tiny splinters cracking,
sliding down the paper like the grit
on foreheads on Ash Wednesday, dust to dust.
No-one talks; the only sounds are gulls,
traffic, that soft whispering
of wood dissolving into hand and wrist,
the long curve of her back, muscles
in the taut neck. Circle
of silence, each intent on catching
something elusive, without words or art
we re-arrange its absence, all lines crossed.
Deep in the hush I scribble the long hair
over the impossibilities of her ear.

II

Fast poses. Everyone hurries. Marks
go hard and long, from neck
right down to ankles.
We feel bold. This is art.

Before we're satisfied she moves
again, crouches like a runner,
hands on floor, head eager.
Discarded torsos are tossed on chairs.

For Michelangelo this was the soul
— thews, biceps, muscled turn of shoulder.
For a second I remember
his pietá behind its cold glass panel,

limp head flung back, life gone,
eyes closed. The woman looking down.

III

She isn't perfect but she's beautiful;
a thousand veins and sinews, a miracle.

Lucy's in her slumber on the mattress,
her body a problem now for someone else,

its angles and shadows, proportions
that won't match, drawn and redrawn

over and over. And out there, in hospitals,
on beaches, benches, begging in subway halls,

under the dirt and disease and worries,
caked-on emotion and old bruises,

they're all like this, Eve in her innocence,
the old untouched under their broken veins.

"Take a break" the tutor says.
We rub her dust from our dark fingers.

IV

Talking to Lucy in the coffee break
is bizarre, all surface,
about the weather, nowhere here to park.

I know this woman's body like no other,
all its intimate creases,
the way the stomach hangs, the fingers'

complexities. I've studied its hollows,
seeing from week to week
how the skin's hues alter. Now

her speech is a shock, as if some still life
spoke, a landscape turned its head.
I don't know her surname, where she lives,

anything about her. All the world
might be like this. Seen, not understood.

V

We try candlelight. All shadows change;
room suddenly small, breaths and draughts
and flickers. The body dissolves to a net of darknesses,
hollows, never still.
                    Once in Rome I saw
the Capuchins' grim joke at death's excesses;
ornate baroque decor all made of bones,
clocks and hourglasses and cornices,
whole skeletons in habits. Death's inside;
you can't draw it but it's there, maybe this
cell, that breast, that memory.
Limp head slumped, chest fallen still,
what was different gone so slow you never saw it.

Dirty curtains rattle. Pain and sun come back.
We see what a mess we've made.

Artist, Neath Abbey

In the sun I watch you, in the web of stone,
the ruin about you like a tilted dream;
tracery of moss on arch and pinnacle,
lichen, with its tiny uncurled fronds;
textures of prayer, all innocent of language,
spindly as ogham, and as meaningful.

Squatting there among the lost blue windows
the past in your fingers opens an arch of light,
and we laugh, because the craft's back in the valley;
somehow all the makers have come home,
putting the wood's heart to its oldest uses,
praising, conjuring, making marks on time;

letting it speak what poetry can't speak
— a precision of form, slow curve of a line —
taking the rose of glass out of the heart
and splashing it wide across the dirty paper;
learning lessons of light, the spaces beyond faith,
as the monk learned them, bending as you bend.

At the Villa Borghese

I

For half an hour she's cleaned that forehead,
rubbed tiny intricate circles in the dirt
till the flush comes, as if he felt her. She warms
him, brings light to his eye. Delicate
swabs and then her finger on his lips;
he's smiling, coyness coming out of shadow.
Foolish, I look past them through the window.

She makes him laugh, vine leaves askew,
and all the time her concentration holds
through fidgets and the shifting of cramped limbs.
Does she think of him, or even see him
in the grains of pigment, crusted varnishes;
his smirk, the smudge in his uplifted hand
that might be a spilling wine-glass, or a weapon?

II

Cramped among marble I'm turning cold,
rigid, my mind gone hard and smooth.
Sometimes I dream of you, your face
under my fingers, looming out of time;
an afternoon of effort on one earlobe,
fixing flakes of skin, dissolving
all my forebears' jealousies.
You knew them too, contorted here
as others will be when my hands are bone.
Whoever painted you, we make you ours,
patch by patch, nothing left untouched,
and only we know, close-up, what you are;
construct of smear and scumble and impasto,
all your secret layers worn so thin
we can see right through you.

III

I was painted to be stared at.
Look through the decay
that flakes me, powders my
limbs, obscures with fine
film all you see of me.

I'm yours but you never know
how; wear yourselves out
till somehow from streaks
and brushstrokes here I am.
I never turn out as you hope.

You can't ignore me either,
your thoughts on me
endlessly, your fingers
down the centuries at work.
You can't leave me alone;

Like a mirror
I'm your arrogance,
your own face in the dark.
You've mastered nature but not me.
I cost you lives. And lives.

Mr Bucknall's Skeleton

Marlborough Downs, 1906

Not mine. A woman's from a barrow at Manton.
I watched as they tweezered the fibres of shroud;
shale, amber, fragments of gold.
Her bones were tossed and huddled in rubble,
flint-white; stones of a broken henge, all blunt
and rounded. Under her wrinkles
she'd always been smooth as the downs,
some matriarch, frail and imperious,
chalky with arthritis, gnarled hands open now,
wide as a child's.
                The skull lay on its side;
huge, overgrown, I walk on it;
it's Overton Hill, Hackpen Ridge.
I've stumbled in its slants and hollows.
Sheep make trails, thoughtless, down its forehead.

That's why I took her home, a pile of pieces,
till her memory shrivelled
and I gave away her finger-bone.
Days later the pain tightened round my own.

Her ring, vengeful, white as leprosy.

Deep in the barrow,
clumsy with the spade, I put her back,
and as a gift my amputated finger,
the tiny bones lost instantly in dust,
so I couldn't tell hers or mine or earth's,
not any more, under our green skin.

But sometimes I know I'm turning cold as a hillside,
riddled with cracks, curled in a porous sleep;
the rain seeping into my dreams.

Bryn-Celli-Ddu

Go there early, crossing
fields, scattering sullen sheep.
Go the way the makers would have come,
up the clogged stream.
The woman's on the green mound, sitting.
The gate's click makes her look up.

Widdershins, circle the tomb. At the crack
scramble down the passage to the chamber
empty at the heart
like every grave. Silent,
watch her walk away along the track.
In the dark you'll wonder

what she found here in the barrow,
entering the underworld like a heroine
in a hollow hill.
She looks familiar.
Is it that you've somehow
followed Orpheus, have come in

to her soil and earth,
into the darkness early,
that confrontation that the world finds hard;
asking as a poet should, the word
where no words are? Is this myth,
without its stories and its certainties?

Cromlech

Ridged like the sea's back,
like the moon's profile pitted, cratered;
cupmarked with mosses, bone-grey;
creature turned fossil, craving drink.

Crouched before it, crawling in it, arms full of dark,
I feel its weight poised, grinding the uprights,
crushing antler, rammed chalk, down to the powdered
bone. I asked not to feel this and haven't,

till now, palms in the soft mud;
ravenously swallowed. Eaten whole.
Like them I bring my dead here cleaned to memory,
without speech, fleshless, seen only in sleep.

This could be any time; the may spilling
white in the grass; rain down fingers,
down the spine of the stones; taken at their word
someone crouching here, between claws.

Fimbulwinter

Sweating between towns on country roads
you learn your place. The hedge,
the slip-stream, the exhaust.
You shouldn't be walking here, have no right;
read in exasperated glances and close shaves
your offence, though all the pilgrims, pedlars,
vagabonds in you rise up and spit.
Sidling to a bend you hold your breath
and the rucksack tight. Lorries roar
like dragons. Hawthorn shrivels,
each leaf a frenzy of dust.

These are the only roads
to where you need to go, a *via dolorosa*
between hedgerows where no buses run
and no-one stops, and where no voices are.
A gate's relief. You trespass in the grass,
see how we've shrunk our comings and our goings
to grey intent, shortest way
between two points, the land
by-passed, all stories left untold.

Maybe it's come closer than we think,
that time of no compassion for each other;
the wind-age, wolf-age, long destruction
that all cultures fear. Maybe the
monsters have been loosed and no-one noticed.
On Hell's road all men tremble; on this
field's edge the littered hedgerow holds
its stubborn line. There's no protection;
no-one's spoken since you left the town.
The only words are huge, stretch into distance.
Stop, they say. Give way. Give way.

At Bertholey House

"lone white house, symbol of a world of wonder..."
— Arthur Machen

The forest hangs in its uneasy heat.
Bracken bends and whispers, crisp with spore.
A beetle cracks its hot black carapace
uncreasing a glint of wing. Down long
green tracks you walked towards the house

where lizards flicker on the baking arch,
light tasting their deep crevices like tongues.
Broken open by the flames' red fingers
something has escaped. You stood among bees
speaking to me in a haze of thyme.

Candles once, and tasselled red brocade.
Bound books that crackled in the open case.
Your fingers in the charred grit.
A poet's dream, you said, a tower in a tale. When
nothing's left of all our words but light.

Cat Lane

Fog lives here. It slinks against walls,
lithe, muscled, never heard.
A drainpipe ticks in the yard,
each drop wobbling as it falls.

No one in the dark nights of November
comes down here to the overflowing bins.
Wet posters peel softly from palings;
even the rain has claws.

Slot between houses, dark, star-hung,
where the fog prowls for passersby,
rubs against their hearts, gives a sly
cold reminder of its tongue.

The moon's echoes down there shine
like the eyes of ghosts.
A place where memories are lost;
where emptiness comes padding up behind.

Four Fragments for Lent

I

Tithe Barn, Llantarnam

Thickness of walls his outstretched arms;
vines and ivy ripple up his body;
lying deep in leaves, their silence
pattering from the canopy.
Storehouse crammed with green gifts;
over arrowslits, keystone slipping.

What tithes are paid here, offerings
of neglect, lost hours?
They flower and seed, thrust through him,
root and tangle into thorns.
See the weeds unfurl in his hands;
how he welcomes them into his pain.

II
Electric Superstore

In out of the rain, I try to look it.
The same face, enormous, gives me thirty grins,
flickers to thirty pictures of one garden
receding into mist.
I don't know why I'm horrified by this.

Where have they all come from?
Last time I looked machines like these were dreams,
sci-fi, never going to happen.
Already out of date
the future that I haven't even met.

Somewhere a coin rolls and all the screens
go close-up. Thirty glinting pieces.
On the roof the rain drums its reminder.
We've done this.
Whatever we might wish.

III

Rome; Marathon

Men running in narrow streets.
Rain on the cobbles makes them slip,
plasters their vests to their skins.

Running on drains and catacombs,
underground altars, martyrs' bones;
against the clock that throbs in the wrist.

Winners gone too far ahead to see;
miles back, on the Ponte Sisto,
stragglers, hands on hips, white-faced.

All around them the Eternal City,
glimpsed in walls and domes and lost
between breaths, splashes of rain.

Pieta in an alley, briefly crossed.
Outside the walls the bald apostle
deep in the silver crowd at the finishing tape.

IV

Tor

The hill heats us, undresses us;
coat and tie, pullover around waist.
Green maze, treacherous, defying us to learn,
spears our sides, makes us breathless, weak.

Once three men were dragged up here on hurdles.
For them we spread our arms,
wind pinning us back, clouds
blackening the lanes.

Seeing as Richard Whiting saw,
through the sting of our eyes,
a cold remorseless country bleak with spring,
rising to its unrepentant thieves.

Vampire Ballet

The dancer's squirming back. He's on his knees.
Music is a heartbeat, fascination.
The whole theatre's tense. No-one breathes.

It's that other man our eyes are on,
the dark one. Relentless he stalks
us all across the stage. As the music's torn

to pieces see him slither into smoke.
We feed off him, just as he feeds off us;
counting the scenes till he's back,

the wingflap from the crypt, the hiss,
his twisted sort of love straight through our hearts.
What is it about evil with panache

that infects, brings hot blood to the face,
makes the sullen eager, the heated crowd
all down the stairs avoid each others eyes?

Gypsy Horses

If you walk all day there comes a time
when nothing matters. We'd passed that.
Still the daylong drenching rain
came at us like spears till we were numb,
stumbling in ruts. High on the track
trees trickled from their outlines.

Then ahead, the strange dark blotches.
They wandered oddly off the ground,
no clearer as we neared. Fear
slid into our silence; we watched
them blur towards us, dreading what we'd find,
but the mist turned, and they were only horses,

piebald, black and ghost. A crimson
shock of flames, men sitting round on straw,
tarpaulin dripping. We were relieved,
more than we knew. Later, trudging on,
I felt they'd all come back; outlaws
in the greenwood now, and wolves,

gaberlunzies, guizers, mummers;
that chapel in the forest with its hermit;
cattle kneeling in the barn;
dancers with animal heads from door to door.
As if the horses' trickery made me sure;
in the twilight, beyond towns, something remains.

Eilmer of Malmesbury

The books had crazed me. I gathered feathers,
goose and swan, down of sparrows
snagged on hedges. Some of each,
magpie and crow; I was thief and scavenger and hawk,
renewing my zig-zag vigour like an eagle.
Barbs and flights, I preened them,
laid them on wicker frames, fixed with
pitch the quills I would write with now,
on the air, on history; and I climbed the
early morning to its top, up the body's stairs,
hearing far below my heart
pound on its locked door.

High, giddy, I looked out
from fear. Woods and roofs and tiny people
hung from my feet. The sky waited,
its arms wide open, feathered edges rippling.

And I remember, I still strain to keep, that slow
falling outward into joy, the air holding me
as I lay on it, the second of lifting when I knew
all truths, pierced all dreams, screamed
the raw hawk's rage, the sparrow's terror.
　　　　　Then collapse. Tumbled, buffeted down
the stones of the wall, rib to rib; the crumpling
smash of blackness that was earth.

I lived. Not as I used to live.
I had been Icarus, Bladud, all who trusted,
launched themselves out of sanity. Daily
I plummet back into that flight,
knowing what birds and angels know,
falling through God's fingers, endlessly.

The Thicket

Cutting the brambles, slicing them through,
stalks oozing juice, spent berries
crushed in the mulch underfoot. Deep in dew,
tangled, the travellers-joy hugging me,
seed and fluff and pips in my hair,
I struggle like Michael with the soul's fear.

And it welcomes me, I'm part of it,
webbed, ensnared, till the stems
are sheared, bindweed split
to let sky in, and the lost sun comes.
Dark dreams slink off like spiders.
Beyond leaves, a glint of river.

Blodeuwedd

When oak, I was unbending;
would never have stooped to this.
A thousand years' slow circles
rang from my heart's wood.
Through acorn and gall I saw you
stumble into the world.

When I was broom I was golden;
my spines the haunt of birds.
I hid nothing, had no guile;
wind and rain speared through me.
In tapestries I blossomed
between unicorn and lady.

When meadowsweet, I was innocent;
white froth of fields that are gone.
Spume of hedge uprooted,
of scent and butterflies.
Children and lovers watched Spitfires
through my creamy skies.

What have you made of me, wizards?
Out of me what have you formed?
Treacherous, a taloned hunter,
mutated into your fall.
The conditions that will cause death;
how is it I know them all?

Re-enactment

He's still wearing the watch, he notices.
There's nowhere to put it now, no time.
He slips it off and hides it in the bushes.

Marching, and the crowd have heard the cornu,
they're turning, taking pictures. Shield
is heavy, slatted lorica locks him straight.

Families on the ruins of their past.
He demonstrates the pilum, the short sword,
thinking the moment might be now. Or now.

A thousand clocks, unnoticed, twitch towards it;
home in the empty house the rooms all ticking;
the glint in the hedge. Find some interest,

they'd said, get out; and so he had, marching
into history each weekend, away
from the house and the dust on the wardrobe door.

Now he re-enacts a silent battle,
cranking up the onegar, jerking it free,
the ball soaring, thudding in the bank

and he loves it when the children gasp.
Maybe now, this is the moment. Or when
he hoists the shield for the testudo,

the final charge towards the stand,
the kids screeching, the women laughing down,
maybe it was then, the moment her fingers loosed.

A year, a thousand, what's the difference?
The past is past, will never be brought alive.
Except like this, this photograph, the boy

trying on the helmet, struggling with the shield.
Somewhere though, the moment lies in wait
He'll wear the armour home under his coat.

Estuary Poems

Fil súil nglais
fégbas Éirinn dar a hais;
nocho n-aicceba íarmo-thá
firu Érenn nách a mná.

I

Under the stars they come ashore all night,
wading chest-high through the lights of Weston.
In the dark the current scoops and sleeks;
acres of scored mud plipping quietly.
See them flounder, waist-deep, long skirts dragging,
sick with the bilge-stink and hunger;
the river mocks them with its dangerous *croeso*,
the sucking pools, the children handed up,
lethal tidewash, wet caress,
fingers clutched in the soil and stones,
till the bank is firm and the land forms,
and they sit on the saltmarsh and slither into their shoes.

Cheaper than ballast, dumped in the dark.
Never uprooted from the memory's mud.

II

Not much of it then. Not even attached to the town,
a village of shanties, brothels, beerhouses on the dock,
and the ships, ships from everywhere, and the earth
coal. It was a warren they slipped into,
the crowded houses, stevedores and stokers,
sail-makers, lodgers, carpenters and thieves.
Babel of languages, loud confusion,
where people clung to those they knew, fearing
the knife in the street, the drunken scream;
somewhere a whistle playing reels.
A place like Purgatory on the marsh,
unstable, erupting in riot, the long grey
hills of cinders gritty underfoot.
And the river, taking its share, taking its payment.

III

It shouldn't have been like this. Maybe
Maggie O'Neil in her room among the clothes
and children crying would have known the story;

the sea green as glass, the white birds,
the boat of heroes skipping on the waves,
and the island, when they came to it, a burst

of sorcery, no sorrow there, no sickness,
but music and the long sweet centuries
of sunlight in the cool rooms of the palace.

They'd faced away from that, turned east;
I wonder if that made her feel afraid, the broken
line, the child who'd lost the promise of the poets.

Rocking him in the dark, the dingy kitchen,
counting how much the final turn had taken.

IV

In a photo someone showed me once
they're digging the foundations;
men in shirt-sleeves, with picks and barrows,
looking grim. I have the names but don't know
who to fit them to, which might be Patrick Hurley
or James Williams. Maybe none. They
dug deep, whoever, deep in the costly land,
dreaming the parables of rock and sand,
building the house of souls, raising over
the estuary the spire's reminder.
And in the windows captains laid their names
under the feet of saints.
                        Maybe that Michaelmas
in the silence they felt less unease,
as if they'd made the shore a firmer place.

V

Out in the dark fresh water becomes salt;
two tides join.
                I wonder
how much time it took them to forget,
learning a new country, new weather,
resettling. How many generations
to lose the flavour, mingle with the main,
become diluted imperceptibly,
word by unknown word; the children
coming back with different accents, always
the children first.
                    Home known, home heard of,
home receding into legend, and all the while
unnoticed, this is home, and no-one says it
till the moment's gone, the strange
collective calm decision taken.

VI

Walking back from mass, the Usk reminds us.
Cracked mud like toffee in a tray;
ruined boat rimmed with gulls.
Here's the dry-dock choked with grass
where Peter Rafferty fell in and drowned.
And Gin Jimmy the pilot out from Bristol
under the tangled weed, the green wave.
And if we had a boat we could put out
and sail from here to home
though this is home, not Cork or Cappoquin
or all the places in the family tales.
A man can drown in water or on land,
a people drown a people, gradually,
gently. Without a ripple.

VII

The shop was always dark and smelled of turps.
In the coal fire at the back, newspapers
and ends of anaglypta burned.
My grandfather would stand there, looking out
into the rain; we'd arrange the paint-tins
in their rust rings, and now and again
on the two round chairs old men
would come and sit, umbrellas dripping.

And slowly the streets around fell into ruin,
department store opposite boarded up,
plastered with posters, sprouting weeds.
We watched it happen and made bitter comments.
After a few years no-one noticed it;
children were grown who'd never been inside.

VIII

Decay does that, makes things invisible;
the boarded street you drive down in the bus,
forgotten, something your eyes pass over, people
not quite certain how it was.
And in the shop my grandfather would prophesy
darkly, wrapping the slithering rolls of paper
tight with tape. Tin of size
knocked from a shelf with a stick. Cash in the drawer.
His words have all come true; shops
are warehouses outside the town. No-one listens
to old men. The threads like spiders' webs
that bound us all are breaking one by one.

At half past five, I'd sweep behind the counter,
picking the shilling notes out of the litter.

IX

When do the poets begin their voyages;
when is the coracle lowered
into that river? Under what weir
are they found, the twisters of words?

And the changes that come to them,
blurring from hawk to cat to otter
over the years, as if they're hunting
that exhilaration and that power.

Of all the ingredients in the cauldron only
three drops burn, they sting;
in desk and street and alleyway
no-one will guess that silent inner twisting

or even know the moment when you're born.
The moment when the words all stand in line.

X

They say the Brontes had a box of soldiers;
on those they built their wild exotic kingdoms,
in tiny books barely decipherable
wrote their marriages and histories and wars.
But the key to the box, who brings that home,
how much does it cost? And why can no-one else
unlock it and see everything the same?

In the three-decked galleon of the shop
I rode the seas of formlessness and power,
from the lit windows looking down on shoppers
black on the glossy pavements in the rain.
And just across the street and round the corner
the plaque for W.H. Davies dripped with water,
who'd ridden to nowhere on the thundering trains.

XI

This place is still a Babel; in the streets
voices cry out. Each nation knows its own;
the hieroglyphs of thought, unreadable
except by smile and gesture. Going abroad
is never strange because of this.
                                                        And I,
bred in it, orphan of two languages,
choose from a third the bright
unwieldy glances of the poet.

Thinking of my father home from war,
the words "Céad míle fáilte" on his cake,
piped in icing, and how they ate them,
and the greeting became crumbs. And later,
when the TV spoke in Welsh,
how he'd get up and growl and turn it over.

XII

Was it on the Gaer, or Cwrt-y-defaid
that he sat with her, looking out to sea,
over the islands, the eerie stub
of Brent Knoll? Out there, he said
the Fisher King went sailing in the stories
and dredged a legend up into his nets;
those who taste it never struggle free.
And Tathan with his altar sailed up there
embedding in the estuary's arms, and
Vikings maybe, and long before, the blue-
-stones, bound on rafts, for sorcery.

And so once, years ago, did we, fleeing
the rain, thinking we could bring
all we needed in the cargoes of our hearts.

XIII

In a quiet moment while they're reading
I see behind these children, in this room,
their parents, small and wearing Sixties clothes,
and me among them, swinging my feet;
ink on fingers and the desk too big.

This generation hasn't tasted hunger,
their world bright, computerised;
oblivious of Ireland, the thin
invisible threads that hold us here,
the dead in their hollows in the rain,
the significance of street names.
These are the ones who finally break free.

Though maybe the teachers thirty years ago
stood here and thought the same thing about me.

XIV

Out of sedges, the prow comes silent. Faint
swelling of Usk-water, a ripple. His hand
comes up and I take it; it's cool
with seaweed bracelets like my father's once.
The boat is leaves and cobweb. I offer him
a Silurian stater, an hour one warm July,
jigsaw pieces, letters from my friends. He takes
instead one small scorched photograph. Then
we're away, a ghost-boat off the mud-banks
into the blur of foghorns at Nash Point, mist
of gulls and rain condensing on my face.
"This is the road to Avalon" he says;
and the river laps against the dark horizon,
where the hunger came from, and must go.

Acknowledgements

Some of these poems have previously appeared in the following publications:

Acumen, The New Welsh Review, Planet, Poetry Wales, The Rialto, Scintilla, Drawing Down the Moon (Seren), *Dove-Marks on Stone* (BABEL), *On the Third Day* (Gomer), *The Whispering Room* (Kingfisher).